2

LET'S
Workbook
GO

by
S. Wilkinson
R. Nakata
K. Frazier

Oxford University Press

Unit 1

Trace and write.

Hi, Scott.
How are you?

Fine, thank you.

_____, Andy.

Fine, _____.

Good-bye, Scott.

See you later.

_____, Andy.

Trace and write.

2

Trace and write.

What is this?

It is a desk.

What is that?

It is _____.

What is _____?

It is _____.

a door

a desk

an eraser   a window

3

Check, trace, and write.

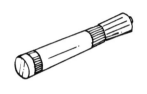  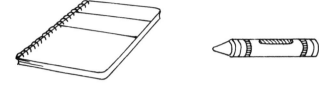

a marker   a book   a notebook   a crayon

Is this a notebook?

☑ Yes, it is.

☐ No, it is not.

Is that a book?

☐ Yes, it is.

☐ No, it is not.

Is _____ a crayon?

Is _____ a marker?

4

Trace and write.

What are these?

They are puzzles.

What are _____?

They are _____.

What are _____?

_____ balls.

What are those?

They are kites.

What are _____?

They are _____.

What are _____?

_____ yo-yos.

5

Trace, check, and write.

Are these cats? Are those dogs?

☐ Yes, they are. ☐ Yes, they are.
☐ No, they are not. ☐ No, they are not.

Are _____ birds? Are _____ frogs?

☐ Yes, they are. _____, they _____.
☐ No, they are not.

Are _____ rabbits? Are _____ spiders?

_____ _____

Trace and write.

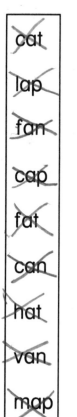

~~cat~~
~~lap~~
~~fan~~
~~cap~~
~~fat~~
~~can~~
~~hat~~
~~van~~
~~map~~

-at   cat   fat   hat

-ap   cap   lap   map

-an   can   van   fan

Circle and write.

van / (fan)

This is a fan .

cap / (map)

That is a map .

cats / (cans)

Those are cans .

(cats) / hats

These are cats .

7

Circle.

this
(that)

this
that

these
those

these
those

Trace and write.

That is an eraser.

are .

are .

Unit 2

Trace.

9

Trace and write.

sick   tired   hot   cold   sad

What is the matter?

I am tired.

I am hot.

I am cold

I am sick

10

Trace and write.

Who is he?

He is Mr. Hill.

He is a cook.

Who is she?

She is Miss Smith.

She is   .

Who is she?

Mrs. Lee.

Who is he?

Mr. White.

a teacher   a taxi driver   a cook   a nurse

Connect, check, trace, and write.

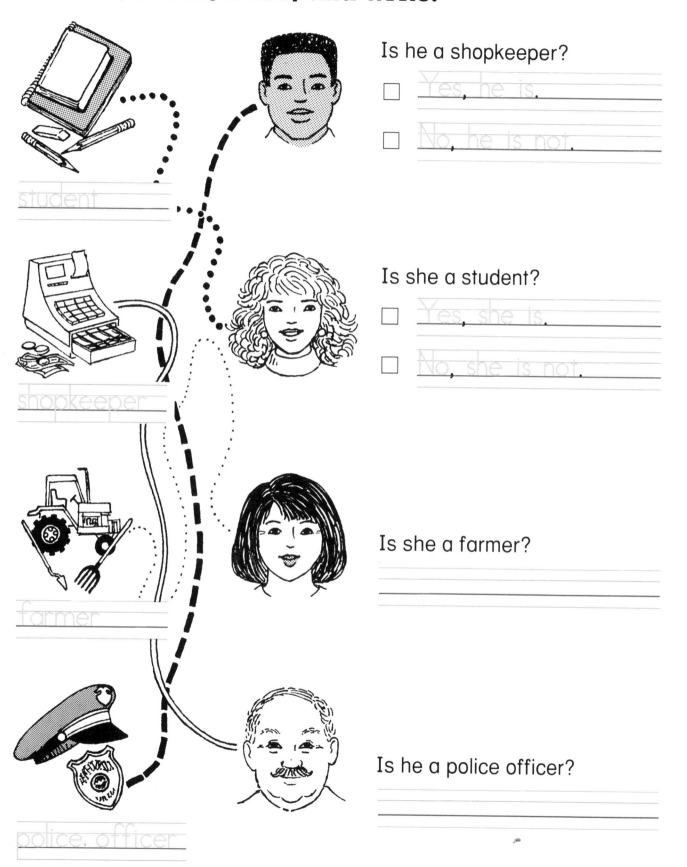

Is he a shopkeeper?

☐ Yes, he is.

☐ No, he is not.

student

Is she a student?

☐ Yes, she is.

☐ No, she is not.

shopkeeper

Is she a farmer?

farmer

Is he a police officer?

police officer

Trace and write.

Who are they?

They are Mr. and Mrs. Lee.

They are teachers.

They are _____

They are _____

_____

_____

_____

_____

| farmers | teachers | cooks | shopkeepers |

Connect and check.

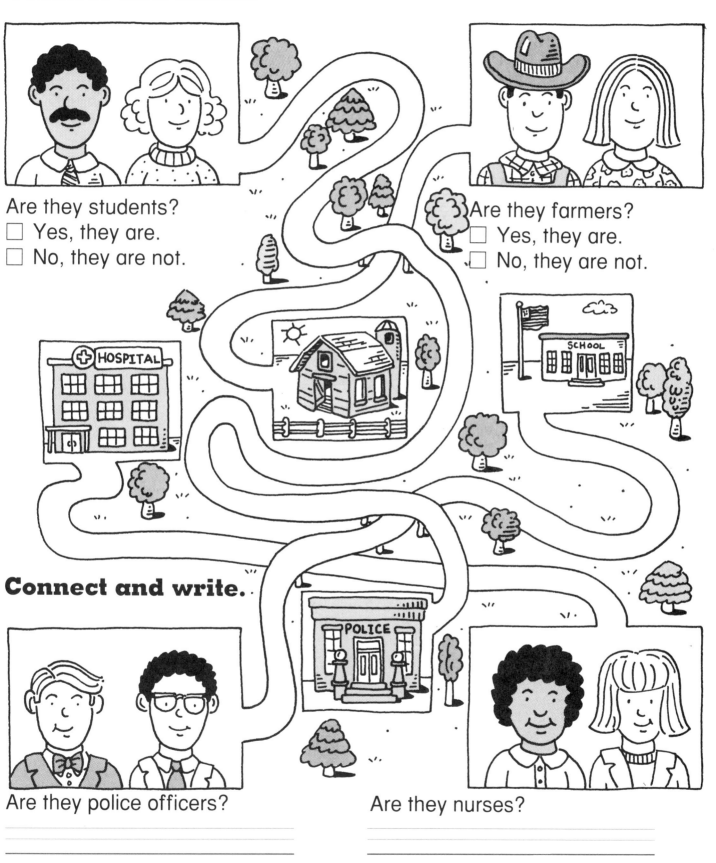

Are they students?

☐ Yes, they are.
☐ No, they are not.

Are they farmers?

☐ Yes, they are.
☐ No, they are not.

Connect and write.

Are they police officers?

Are they nurses?

Trace and connect.

pen

red

Ted

hen

bed

pet

wet

net

ten

-en

-et

-ed

Circle and write.

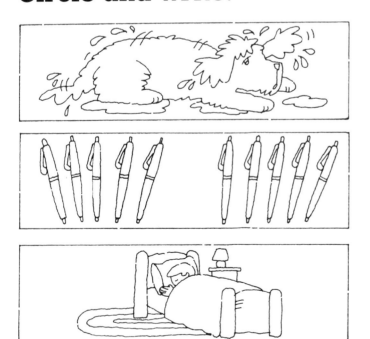

net / pet

The _____ is wet.

pens / hens

They are ten _____.

bed / red

Ted is in the _____.

Circle.

he
she
they

he
she
they

he
she
they

he
she
they

Check.

☐ He is hot.
☐ He is sad.

☐ She is tired.
☐ She is cold.

Check, trace, and write.

He is _____.

☐ a police officer
☐ a taxi driver

She is _____.

☐ a shopkeeper
☐ a nurse

16

Review

1. Write.

Across

2.

6.

Down

1.

2.

3.

4.

5.

7.

```
         1
         ↓
2→ s  t  u  d  e  n  3t      4
↓s                   ↓t      ↓
 h                    t
 o                    t
 p                    t      5
 k                    t      ↓
 e                    t
 e                    t
6→ p           7      ■
 e             ↓
 e
 r
```

2. Circle and write.

He
She
They

_____ is Mr. Hill.

He
She
They

_____ are nurses.

3. Trace and write.

These are pens.

are birds.

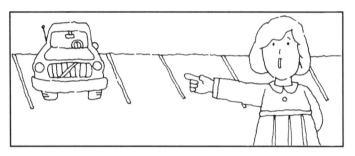

is a car.

4. Trace and write.

She is hot.

He is _____.

_____ is _____.

Unit 3

Trace and write.

Where do you live, Andy?

I live in Hillsdale.

What's your address?

It's 20 South Street.

ANDY NELSON
20 SOUTH STREET
HILLSDALE

Where do you live, Kate?

I live in _____.

What's your address?

It's _____.

KATE HILL
15 MAIN STREET
HILLSDALE

Connect, trace, and write.

What is his telephone number?

It is 231-6544.

What is her telephone number?

It is _____.

What is her telephone number?

_____

What is his telephone number?

_____

414-9051

796-3925

299-7253

231-6544

Write.

What is your telephone number?

_____

Trace.

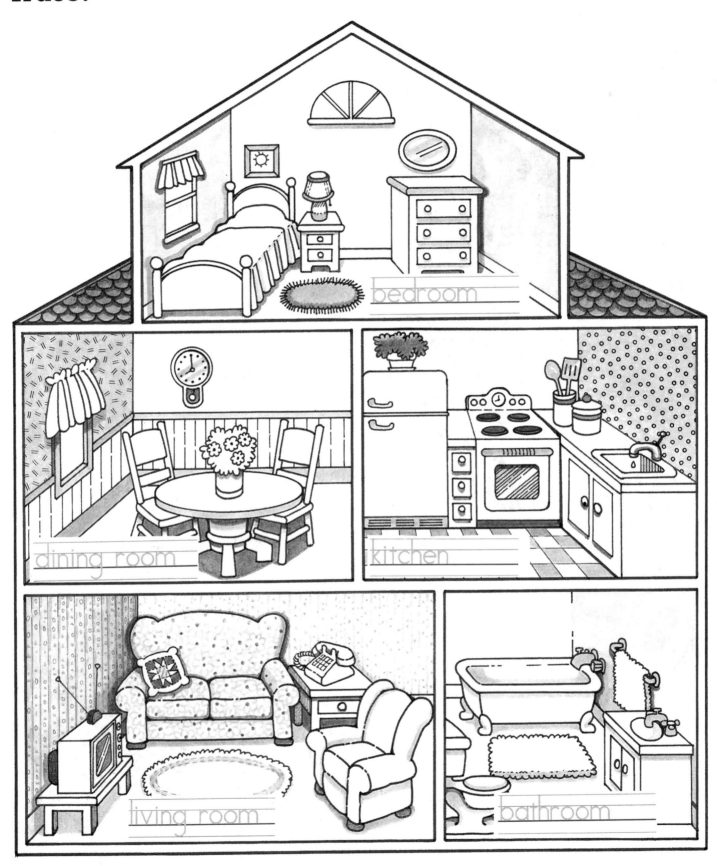

bedroom

dining room

kitchen

living room

bathroom

Trace and write.

Where is the TV?

It is in the living room.

Where is the bathtub?

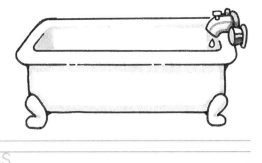

It is _____.

Is the refrigerator in the kitchen?

Yes, it is. _____

Is the stove in the bedroom?

_____

Where is the bed?

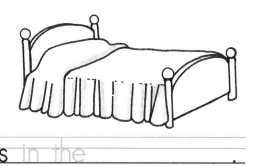

It is in the _____.

Where is the sink?

_____

Is the lamp in the bathroom?

No, it is not. _____

Is the sofa in the living room?

_____

22

Trace.

behind

in front of

on

Trace and write.

There is a cat   behind the sofa.

There is a table in front the sofa.

There are flowers on   the table.

next to

in

under

Check and write.

Is there a window behind the bed?

☐ Yes, there is.

☐ No, there is not.

Is there a door next to the bed?

_____

_____

Are there cats in the bed?

☐ Yes, there are.

☐ No, there are not.

Are there bags under the bed?

_____

_____

Trace and write.

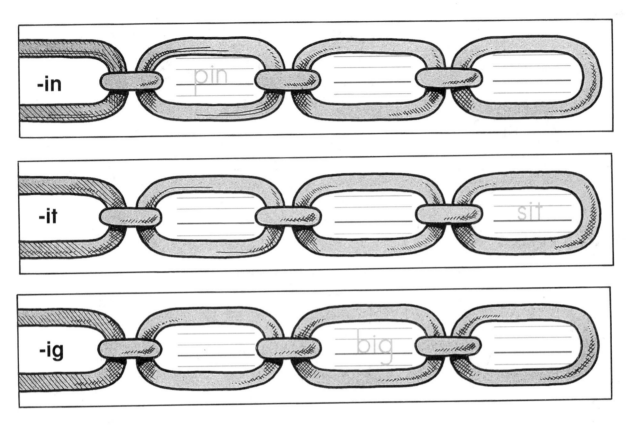

-in

pin

-it

sit

-ig

big

pin
pit
fig
twig
fin
hit
sit
big
thin

Circle and write.

pin / fin

This is my thin _____.

fig / twig

This is my big _____.

hit / sit

I can _____ in the pit.

25

Circle.

in front of
behind

under
next to

next to
behind

under
in front of

Match.

bed
sink
refrigerator
sofa ————————————— living room
toilet   dining room
telephone   kitchen
stove   bedroom
TV   bathroom
bathtub
lamp

Write.

The _____ is in the _____ .

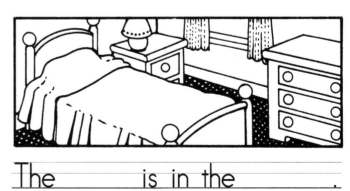

The _____ is in the _____ .

Unit 4

Trace and write.

bag   notebook   pencil   eraser

Trace and write.

He cannot find his pencil.

She cannot reach the bookshelf.

He cannot _____.

She cannot _____.

Trace and write.

Look at him!   Look at   !   Look at   !

Trace and write.

He can _____.

She can _____.

He can _____.

sing a song   use chopsticks   ride a pony

29

Trace and write.

What can he do?

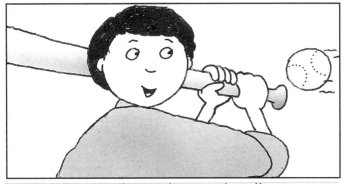

He can play baseball.

What can she do?

She can sing a song.

do a magic trick.

ride a bicycle.

Draw, trace, and write.

What can you do?

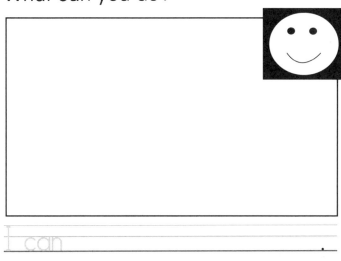

I can _____ .

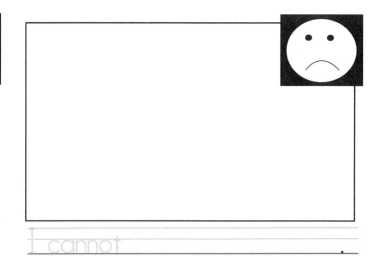

I cannot _____ .

30

Circle.

She can / cannot sing a song, but she can / cannot dance.

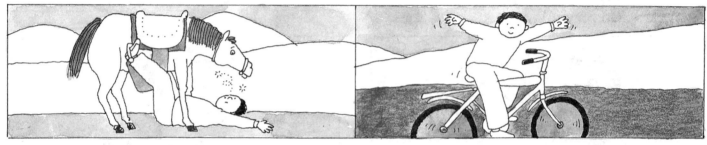

He can / cannot ride a pony, but he can / cannot ride a bicycle.

He can / cannot swim, but he can / cannot climb a tree.

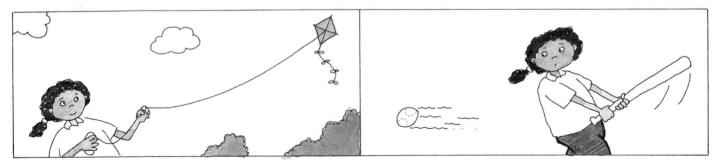

She can / cannot fly a kite, but she can / cannot play baseball.

Trace and write.

Can she speak English?

Yes, she can.

Can he play with a yo-yo?

No, he cannot.

Can he draw a picture?

Can she swim?

Write.

Can you ride a bicycle?

Can you sing a song?

Yes, I can.
No, I cannot.

Trace and write.

dog
run
top
sun
frog
stop
fun
mop
log

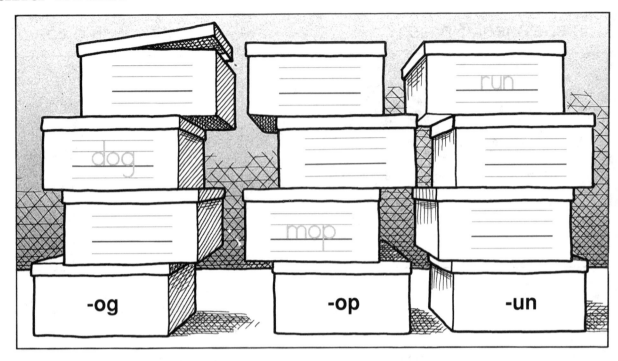

-og **-op** **-un**

Circle and write.

run/fun   fun/sun

She can _____ in the _____.

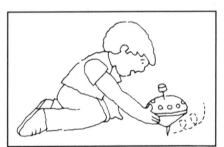

sun/stop   top/mop

I can _____ the _____.

dog/frog   log/dog

The _____ is on the _____.

Circle, trace, and write.

me
him
her

can
cannot

Look at _____ I _____ She _____ fly a kite.

me
him
her

can
cannot

Look at _____ I _____ He _____ sing.

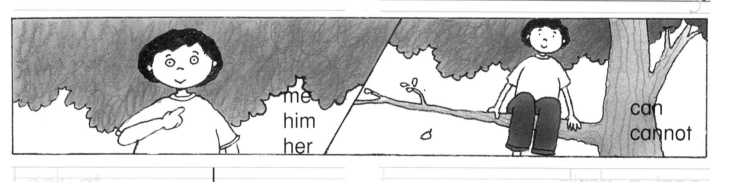

me
him
her

can
cannot

Look at _____ I _____ climb a tree.

Write.

_____ can _____ , but _____ cannot _____ .

Review

1. Unscramble the words.

kins

sink

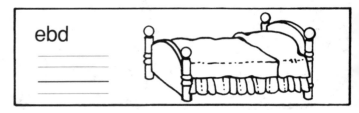

ebd

_____

fsoa

_____

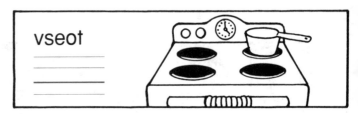

vseot

_____

2. Trace and write.

Across

3.

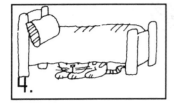

4.

5.

6.

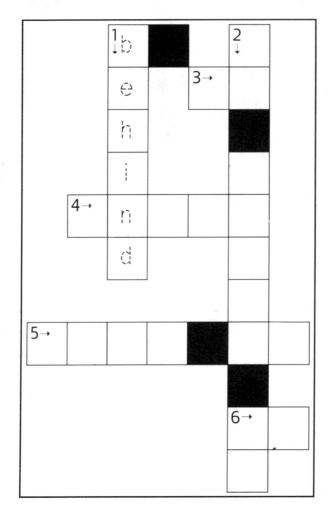

Down

1.

2.

35

3. Circle.

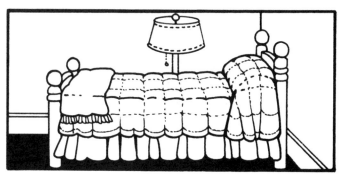

There is/are books on/under the chair.

There is/are a lamp behind/next to the bed.

4. Trace and write.

He can play the piano.

ride a bicycle.

use chopsticks.

sing a song.

Unit 5

Trace and write.

Write.

Do you like spaghetti?

_____

Do you like pizza?

_____

Do you like ice cream?

_____

Do you like cake?

_____

Do you like chicken?

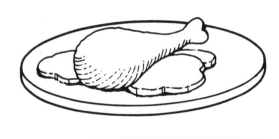

_____

Do you like fish?

_____

| Yes, I do.   No, I do not. |

Circle, trace, and write.

What does ^{he} _{she} want?

<u>She</u> **wants** a hamburger.

What does ^{he} _{she} want?

_____ wants _____.

What does ^{he} _{she} want?

_____ wants _____.

What does ^{he} _{she} want?

_____ wants _____.

| a salad   an egg   a hamburger   an orange |

39

Check.

Does he want a sandwich?

☐ Yes, he does.
☐ No, he does not.

Does she want a salad?

☐ Yes, she does.
☐ No, she does not.

Write.

Does she want an egg?

_____
_____

Does he want a banana?

_____
_____

Connect, trace, and write.

What does he like?

What does she like?

He likes hot dogs.

She likes _____.

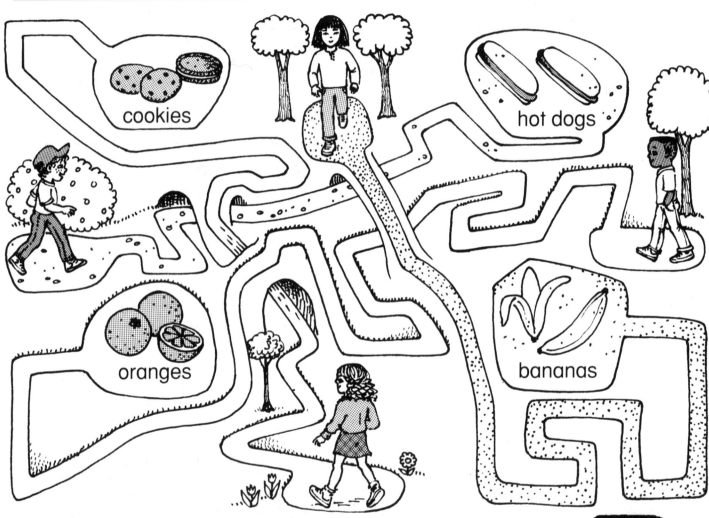

cookies

hot dogs

oranges

bananas

What does she like?

_____ likes _____.

What does he like?

Trace and write.

Does she like hamburgers?

Yes, she does.

Does he like oranges?

No, he does not.

Does he like sandwiches?

Does she like hot dogs?

Write.

Do you like salads?

Do you like cookies?

Yes, I do.   No, I do not.

42

Trace and write.

make
gray
game
crayon
snake
same
play
name
cake

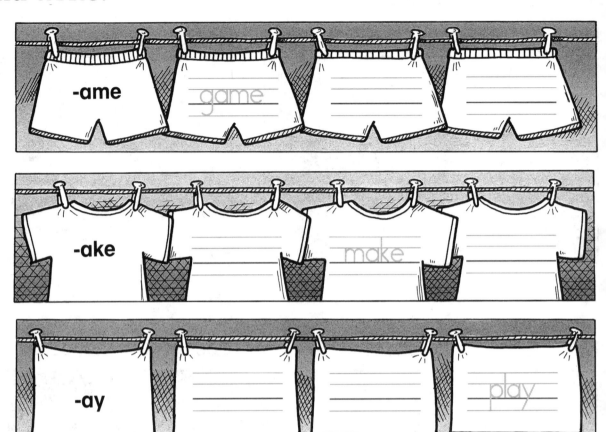

-ame   game

-ake   make

-ay   play

Circle and write.

names / games

These _____ are the same.

cake / snake

I can make a _____.

crayons / cake

Play with the gray _____.

Trace and write.

a salad

an egg

cookie

orange

banana

hot dog

Circle.

He   want   a cookie.
     wants cookies.

She   want   a banana.
      wants bananas.

They want   hamburgers.
     wants sandwiches.

She   want an orange.
     wants an egg.

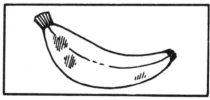

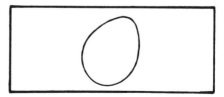

44

Unit 6

Trace and write.

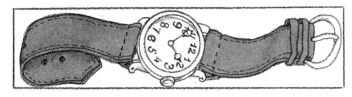

Whose watch is it?

It is Andy's watch.

Whose watch is it?

It is _____ watch.

Whose watch is it?

It is _____ watch.

Kate

John

Andy

Check and write.

Is it John's watch?

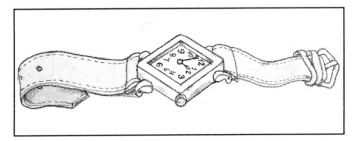

☐ Yes, it is.
☐ No, it is not.

Is it Kate's watch?

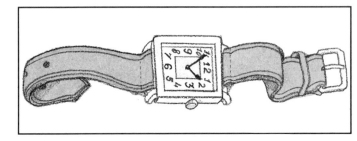

_____

_____

45

Trace and write.

Ted   Sue   Bob

Whose books are they?

Whose notebook is it?

They are Bob's books.

It is _____.

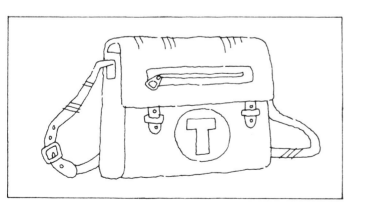

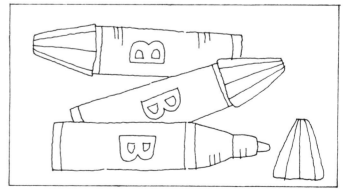

_____ Ted's bag.

_____ Bob's markers.

46

Trace and write.

What do you have in your bag?

I have a comb.

I have _____.

a brush   a comic book
a candy bar   a comb

Draw and write.

What do you have in your bag?

_____

Trace and write.

Do you have a coin in your bag?

Yes, I do.

Do you have a key in your bag?

a tissue in your bag?

48

Connect, trace, and write.

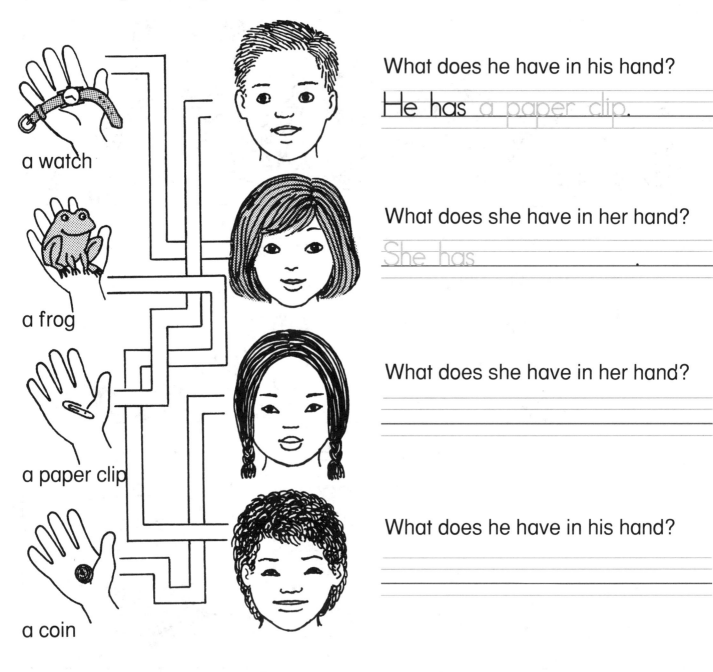

a watch

a frog

a paper clip

a coin

What does he have in his hand?

He has a paper clip.

What does she have in her hand?

She has _____ .

What does she have in her hand?

_____

_____

What does he have in his hand?

_____

_____

Draw, trace, and write.

What do you have in your hand?

I have _____ .

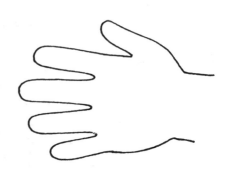

49

Trace and write.

Does he have a book in his bag?

No, he does not.

Does she have a tissue in her bag?

Yes, she does.

Does he have a frog in his bag?

Does she have a ball in her bag?

Write.

Do you have a notebook in your bag?

50

Trace and connect.

ice cream

tree

eat

he

she

green

me

read

sleep

-ea-

-ee-

-e

Circle and write.

eat / read

She can ____ ice cream.

tree / green

The bird sleeps in the ____.

he / me

Look at ____!

51

Trace and write.

He has a watch.

We have crayons.

I a comic book.

She .

Trace and write.

Whose book is it?

It is Tom's book.

Whose pens are they?

They are pens.

Whose crayons are they?

They are crayons.

Whose bag is it?

It is bag.

Review

1. Circle, trace, and write.

She wants a hamburger.

— a banana
— a hamburger

She _____

— an egg
— a salad

_____

— a sandwich
— a hot dog

2. Circle.

orange

banana

hot dog

sandwich

egg

salad

hamburger

cookie

s	x	o	q	b	f	d	z	w	c	o	o	k	i	e
h	a	m	b	u	r	g	e	r	x	o	g	h	r	g
j	e	l	i	t	a	s	v	l	h	o	t	d	o	g
e	p	b	a	n	a	n	a	f	m	b	r	c	n	c
o	s	a	n	d	w	i	c	h	o	r	a	n	g	e

53

3. Connect, trace, and write.

He likes hot dogs.

She likes _____.

_____

4. Circle, trace, and write.

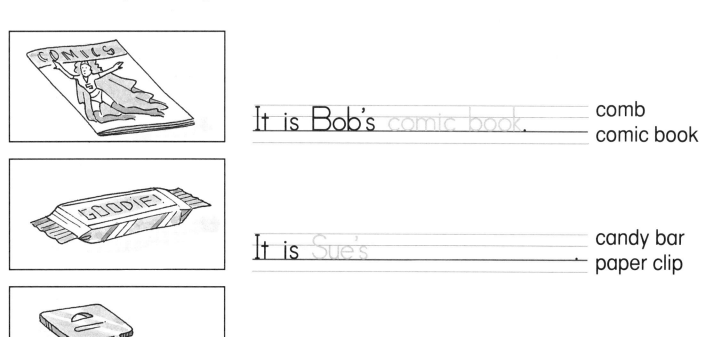

It is Bob's comic book.

comb
comic book

It is Sue's _____.

candy bar
paper clip

It is the teacher's _____.

key
coin

Unit 7

Trace and write.

What time is it?

It is one o'clock.

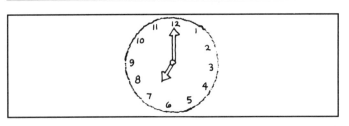

It is ten o'clock.

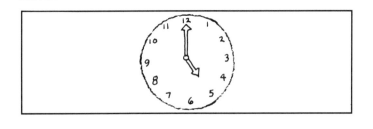

It is ___ o'clock.

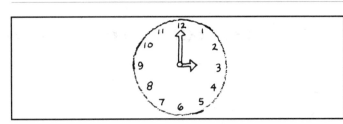

It is ___ o'clock.

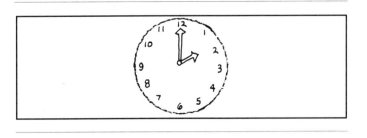

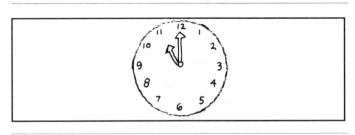

| one | three | five | seven | nine | eleven |
| two | four | six | eight | ten | twelve |

55

Connect.

8:00	twelve o'clock	time for dinner
12:00	nine o'clock	time for school
6:00	eight o'clock	time for lunch
9:00	six o'clock	time for bed

Trace and write.

What time is it?

It is eight o'clock.

It is time for school.

It is _____.

It is _____.

Write and check.

What time is it?

_____

Is it time for bed?
☐ Yes, it is.
☐ No, it is not.

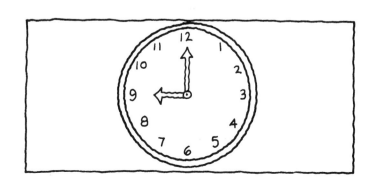

Trace and write.

My Morning

I get up.

I _____.

| wash my face | brush my teeth | eat breakfast |
| get up | get dressed | comb my hair |

Check and write.

 in the morning    in the afternoon

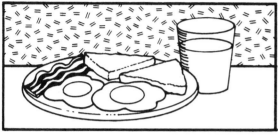

Do you eat breakfast in the morning?
☐ Yes, I do.
☐ No, I do not.

Do you watch TV in the morning?
_____
_____

Do you play the piano in the afternoon?
_____
_____

Do you do your homework in the afternoon?
_____
_____

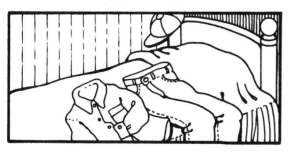

Do you get dressed in the afternoon?
_____
_____

Trace and write.

morning
afternoon
evening
night

What does he do in the morning?

He eats breakfast.

What does she do in the afternoon?

She _____ .

What does she do in the evening?

What does he do at night?

| watches TV | talks on the telephone | studies English | combs her hair |
| plays the piano | eats breakfast | takes a bath | plays baseball |

59

Check.

Does she take a bath in the afternoon?
☐ Yes, she does.
☐ No, she does not.

Does he play baseball in the afternoon?
☐ Yes, he does.
☐ No, he does not.

Write.

Does he take a bath at night?

_____
_____

Does she talk on the telephone in the evening?

_____
_____

Check and write.

Do you study English in the evening?
☐ Yes, I do.
☐ No, I do not.

Do you watch TV at night?

_____
_____

Connect and trace.

Circle and write.

ice / rice

White mice like _____.

nine / pine

The kite is in the _____ tree.

kite / line

Write on the _____.

61

Trace and write.

He _____ baseball in the afternoon.

She _____ breakfast in the morning.

They _____ English in the evening.

They _____ TV at night.

play	eat	study	watch
plays	eats	studies	watches

Unit 8

Trace and write.

What are you doing?

I'm brushing my teeth.

wash ⟶ washing
brush ⟶ brushing
comb ⟶ combing

I'm _____ my face.

I'm _____ my hair.

Trace and write.

① head

②
③
④
⑤
⑥
⑦

⑧
⑨
⑩
⑪
⑫
⑬
⑭
⑮

head	finger	eye	hand	leg
knee	arm	mouth	hair	toe
foot	ear	neck	nose	shoulder

64

Trace and write.

What is he doing?

What is she doing?

He is swimming.

She is _____.

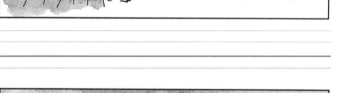

| running | fishing | coloring | swimming | playing | sleeping |

Trace and write.

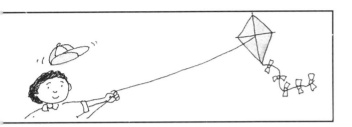

Is he climbing a tree?

No, he is not.

Is she doing her homework?

Yes, she is.

Is she playing the piano?

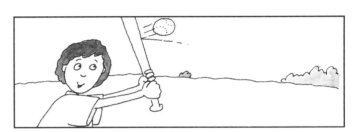

Is he hitting a ball?

Is he riding a bicycle?

Is she playing baseball?

Draw, trace, and write.

What are you doing?

I am   .

Connect, trace, and write.

at school   at home   at the store   at the park

Ted   Meg   Tom   Sue

Where is Ted?

He is at the park.

Where is Meg?

She is _____.

Where is Tom?

Where is Sue?

Trace and write.

What is he doing?

What is she doing?

He is playing baseball.

She is getting dressed.

He is _____ .

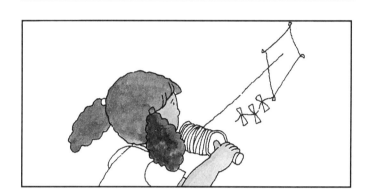

She is _____ .

_____

_____

| flying a kite | playing the piano | getting dressed |
| watching TV | throwing a ball | playing baseball |

Connect and trace.

go   Sue   stone   yo-yo

glue   phone   bone   no   blue

Circle and write.

stone / phone

The dog's bone is by the _____ .

blue / glue

Sue has a _____ yo-yo.

no / go

He can _____ to the store.

69

Trace and write.

Where is he?

He is _____.

Where is she?

She is _____.

Where is she?

_____

Where is he?

_____

at the park   at the store   at school   at home

Write.

Is she running?

_____

Is she eating?

_____

Yes, she is.   No, she is not.

Review

1. Trace and draw.

It is seven o'clock.

It is twelve o'clock.

2. Trace and write.

It is _____.

It is _____.

3. Trace and write.

She plays baseball in the afternoon.

He takes a bath _____.

She gets up _____.

71

4. Circle, trace, and write.

He
She   She is eating.   eating
                                          reading

He   swimming
She   _____ is _____.   fishing

He   watching TV
She   _____ is _____.   studying

He   sleeping
She   _____ is _____.   running

Number Practice

1	one	16	sixteen
2	two	17	seventeen
3	three	18	eighteen
4	four	19	nineteen
5	five	20	twenty
6	six	21	twenty-one
7	seven	22	twenty-two
8	eight	23	twenty-three
9	nine	24	twenty-four
10	ten	25	twenty-five
11	eleven	26	twenty-six
12	twelve	27	twenty-seven
13	thirteen	28	twenty-eight
14	fourteen	29	twenty-nine
15	fifteen	30	thirty

40	forty	70	seventy
50	fifty	80	eighty
60	sixty	90	ninety

100 one hundred

Draw, trace, and write.

1

one   one

2

two

3

three

4

four

5

five

6

six

7

seven

8

eight

9

nine

10

ten

11

eleven

12

twelve

13

thirteen

14

fourteen

15

fifteen

16

sixteen

17

seventeen

18

eighteen

19

nineteen

20

twenty

Count, trace, and write.

21

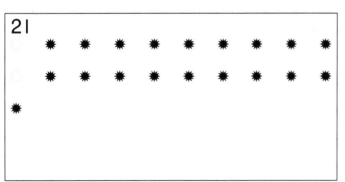

twenty-one

22

twenty-two

23

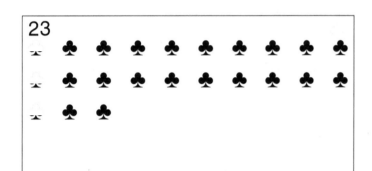

twenty-three

24

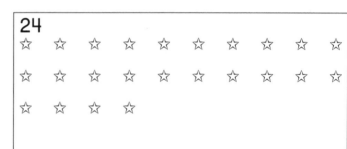

twenty-four

25

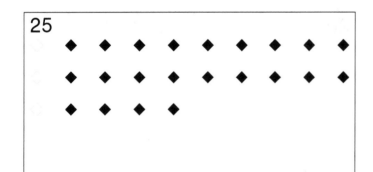

twenty-five

26

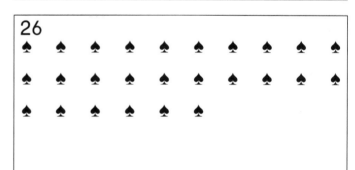

twenty-six

27

twenty-seven

28

twenty-eight

29

twenty-nine

30

thirty

40

forty

50

fifty

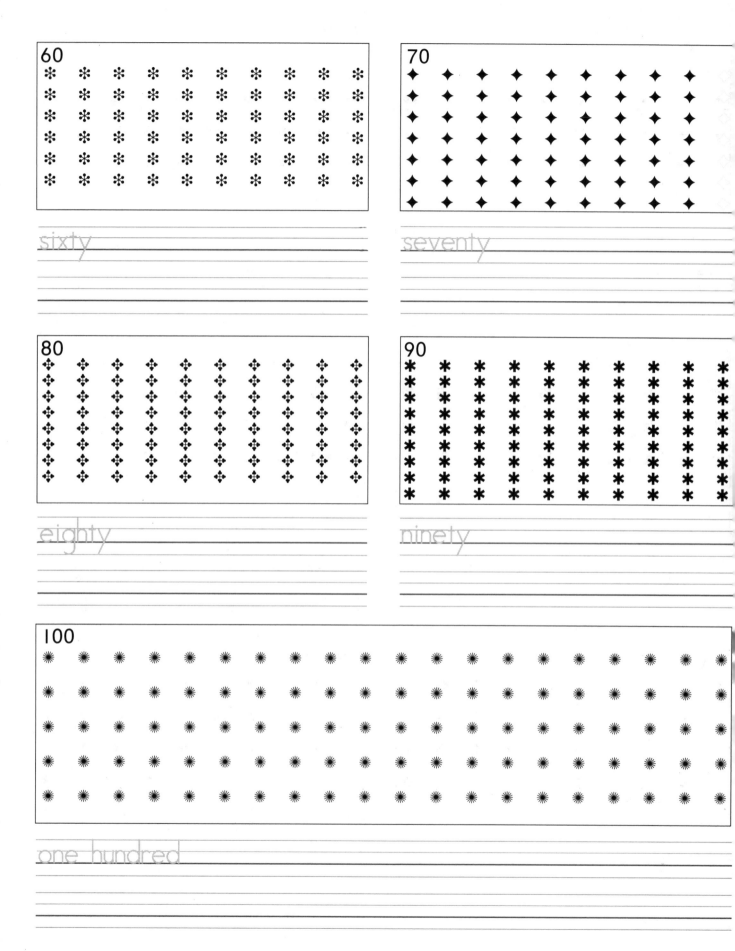

sixty

seventy

eighty

ninety

one hundred

79